Quotes to Stretch Your Brain

by
Susan
Savion

Incentive Publications, Inc.
Nashville, Tennessee

Dedicated to the students of Clary Middle School, Syracuse, New York

Design and Illustrations by Kathleen Bullock
Cover by Robert Voigts
Edited by Jodie Fransen and Marjorie Frank

ISBN 978-0-86530-424-6

2 3 4 5 6 7 8 9 10 13 12

Printed by Sheridan Books, Inc., Chelsea, Michigan • May 2012
www.incentivepublications.com

CONTENTS

Quotes and Activities		Page

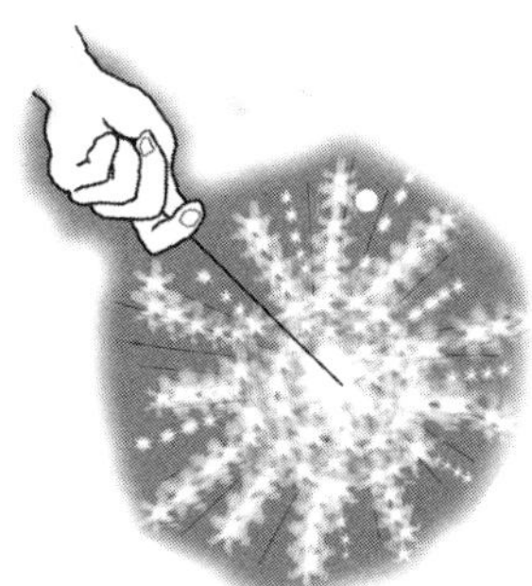

Ignite Critical and Creative Thinking!

An intriguing quote is a spark to stretch the brain! The 55 quotes in this book are specifically chosen to challenge students toward deep reasoning and analysis—toward finding relevance and meaning in each quote. The collection includes wise, witty, inspiring, puzzling, and insightful quotes—each of them with curious nuances that can lead students in different mental directions. Activities encourage them to reflect, internalize or globalize an idea, and to share their ideas with others. Use a quote to start the day or class period, or in any other setting where you'd like to fire up critical and creative thinking.

As You Use the Quotes . . .

- Introduce students to the idea of aphorisms, adages, and proverbs. Ask them to find definitions of these words and share examples.
- The main purpose of the book is to get students to engage with the quote, pushing their thinking to new levels. So be sure to encourage them to look at each quote in different ways and follow where it leads. Be open to the ingenuity and curiosity that can carry students to unexpected interpretations and responses.
- We know from brain research that emotions drive attention, meaning, and memory. So allow students to express fear, opposition, delight, sadness, joy, or humor that may be triggered by these quotes. Make sure students have a chance to share their reflections about the quote.
- Share your own responses to the quotes. Take part in the activities.
- Many quotes, particularly those from the past, use the word "man" or "men" or masculine pronouns. Remind students that the idea applies to all humans.
- When possible, give students an opportunity to learn more about the speakers (or writers) of the quotes. Learn about the place and time in which that person lived, as well as his or her passions, beliefs, and influence on others.
- Consult the Teacher Notes on pages 62 through 64 to find additional information or activities for each quote.
- Don't forget about a quote after the activity is done. Keep quotes posted on the wall for a while. Refer to them. Ask students how a quote from past weeks is affecting them now. Gather these and other quotes in a class quote collection to use for writing experiences and other lessons.

Different Ways to Use the Quotes

Start the class or lesson by reading the quote to students. Also project the quote, feature the quote on the board or on a poster, or give a copy to each student. Introduce the quote, and make sure all the words are understood before students begin other engagement with the quote. Then, use any of these approaches:

- Use a quote as a short inspiration. Share it with students and give them a few minutes to respond and react.
- Use the quote and the activity page as a short warm-up activity. Students can do one, some, or all of the items on the page.
- Use the quote as a springboard for a longer lesson. Most of the pages can be extended to include discussion and sharing of students' written responses.

Topics Covered in the Quotes

Topics	Quotes	Topics	Quotes	Topics	Quotes
Achievement	10	Freedom	34, 36, 39	Poetry, writing	3, 38
Ambition	8, 32, 55	Friendship	6, 45, 52	Progress	41, 51
Appearance	4	Giving and taking	49	Resilience	18
Celebrity, fame	6, 7, 29	Gossip, words	11, 15, 30	Responsibility	34, 48, 50
Confidence	4	Human folly	17, 20, 33	Revenge	37
Doing good	27	Initiative	25, 54	Risk	8, 33, 46
Enemies	1, 45, 52	Jealousy	47	Self-awareness	16, 22, 38, 43
Environment	13	Learning	14	Self-expression	5
Failure	44	Love	46, 55	Secrecy	9
Fashion	43	Money	31	Technology	36
Fear	4, 24, 46	New ideas	23, 24	Teenagers	19, 50
Fools	26, 55	Perception	3, 23	Togetherness	42
Forgiveness	52	Perseverance	12, 18, 21, 28, 44	Wisdom about life	1, 2, 15, 17, 18, 21, 25, 28, 35, 40, 53, 54, 55

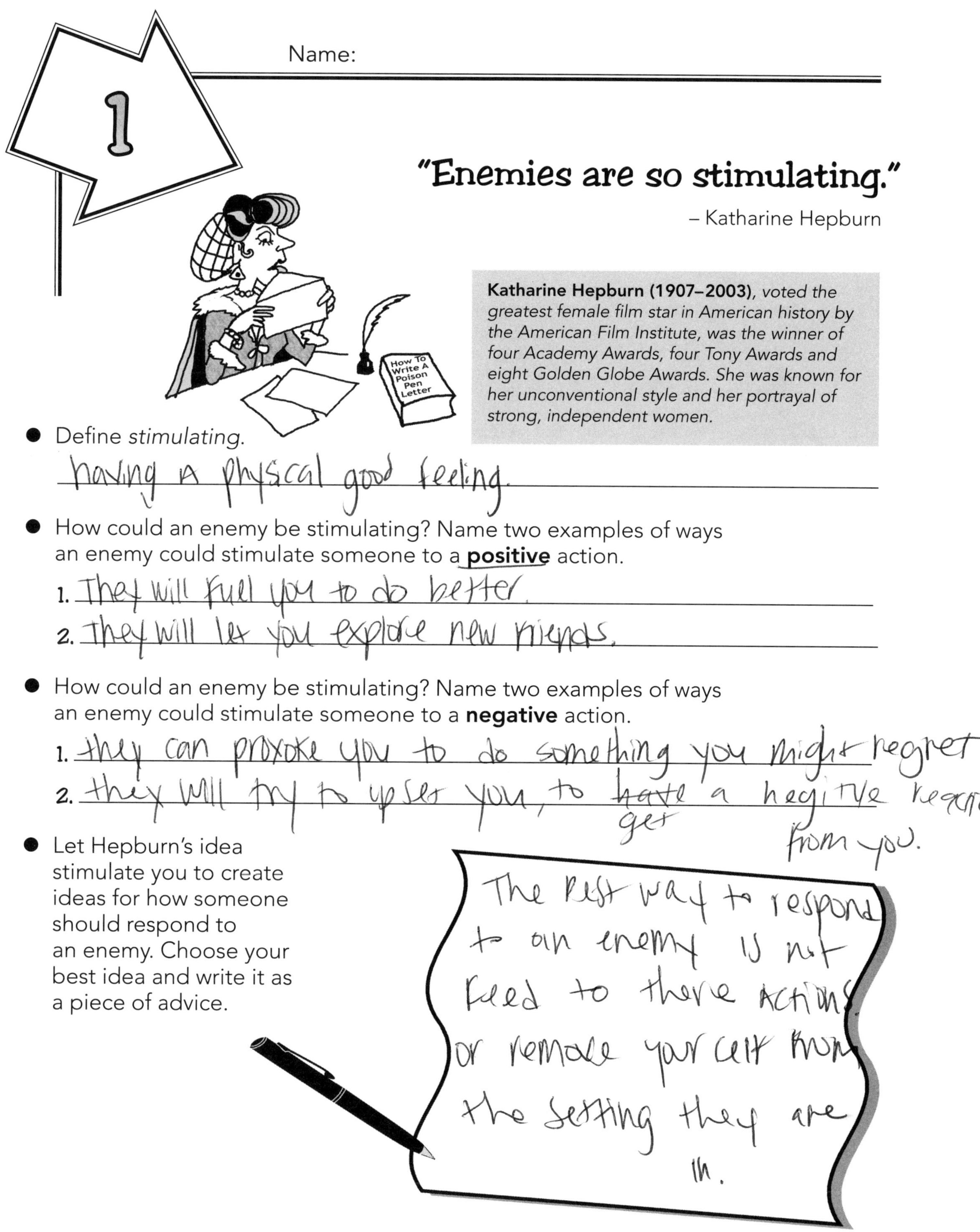

1

Name:

"Enemies are so stimulating."

– Katharine Hepburn

Katharine Hepburn (1907–2003), *voted the greatest female film star in American history by the American Film Institute, was the winner of four Academy Awards, four Tony Awards and eight Golden Globe Awards. She was known for her unconventional style and her portrayal of strong, independent women.*

- Define *stimulating.*

  having a physical good feeling.

- How could an enemy be stimulating? Name two examples of ways an enemy could stimulate someone to a **positive** action.

  1. They will fuel you to do better.
  2. They will let you explore new friends.

- How could an enemy be stimulating? Name two examples of ways an enemy could stimulate someone to a **negative** action.

  1. they can provoke you to do something you might regret
  2. they will try to upset you, to ~~have~~ get a negitive reaction from you.

- Let Hepburn's idea stimulate you to create ideas for how someone should respond to an enemy. Choose your best idea and write it as a piece of advice.

  The best way to respond to an enemy is not feed to there actions. or remove your celf from the setting they are in.

Name: ______________________________

"Life is not having been told that the man has just waxed the floor."

– Ogden Nash

Frederick Ogden Nash (1902–1971) *was one of America's greatest humorists. Before his writing career flourished, he worked as a Wall Street bond salesman, a teacher, and an advertising copyrighter. He wrote children's books, lyrics for musicals, and twenty collections of poems.*

- Do you agree with Ogden Nash's metaphorical statement? ___Idk.___ Tell why or why not.

  ____

- Write your own metaphor to finish the "Life is not . . ." statement.

  Life is not ______________________________.

- Write your own metaphor to finish the "Life is . . ." statement.

  Life is ______________________________.

- Interview three other people about what they believe life is **not**. Ask them to finish the sentence with a metaphor in the style of Ogden Nash's quote. Write their responses. Circle your favorite.

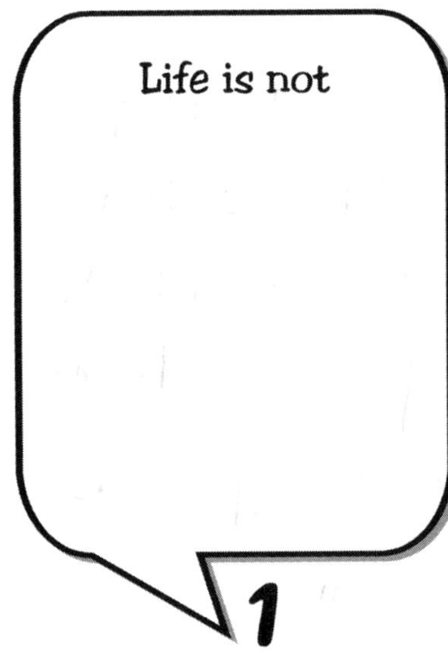

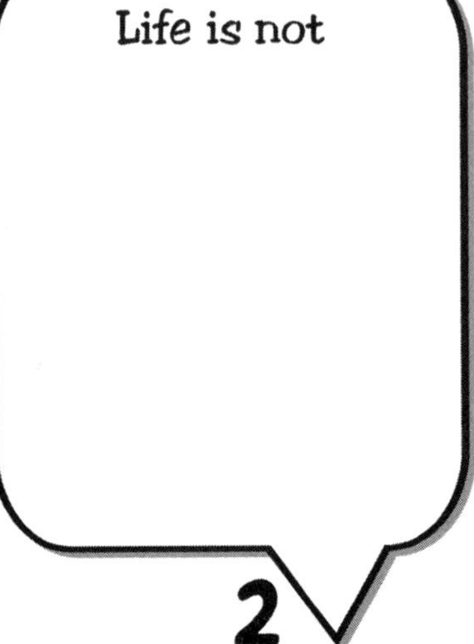

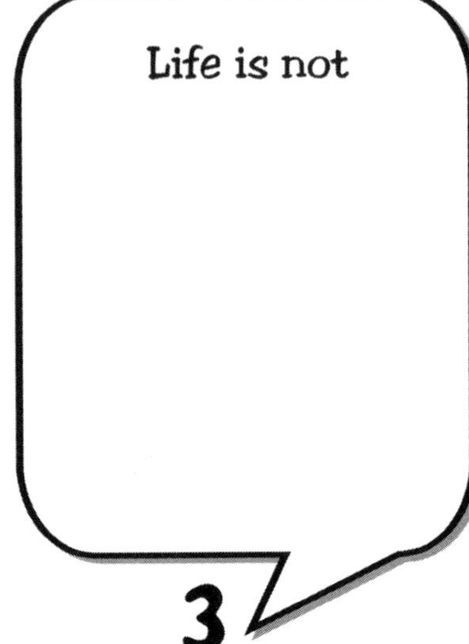

Name: ______________________________

"Writing without passion is stale, flat, lifeless and should be spewed out of the mouth."

– Bruce Coville

- Write a short response to the quote.

____

____

- Rewrite the following sentence with passion.

The dragon jumped down from the building and picked up the girl.

The dragon quickly Jumped down from the building and humidly picked up the girl.

- Coville also wrote, *"Reading is a huge banquet—a smorgasbord, with everything from hamburgers to filet mignon, and a huge sidebar of desserts."* Think about the books you have read as part of a banquet. Name a book that would be . . .

an appetizer. ______________________________

a main course. ______________________________

a dessert. ______________________________

- Explain one of your book choices.

____

____

____

Bruce Coville (1950–) *grew up near the small town of Phoenix, New York. His only regret about those growing-up years is all the time he spent watching television when he could have been reading instead. He did read many books and "zillions" of comic books. When he was eighteen, he started writing children's books. Most of his middle-grade level books are science fiction fantasies, such as* ***The Monster's Ring; My Teacher is an Alien; Sarah's Unicorn; Dragonslayers; Jeremy Thatcher, Dragon Hatcher;*** *and* ***Aliens Ate My Homework****. He has also adapted Shakespeare plays, including* ***Romeo and Juliet*** *and* ***The Tempest*** *for young people. He has authored about 70 books and three musicals for young people. His wife Katherine illustrated several of his books.*

Name: ______________________________

"It's hard to lead a cavalry charge if you think you look funny on a horse."

– Adlai E. Stevenson

Adlai E. Stevenson (1900–1965), *one of the greatest political speakers of his time, was known for his intelligence, eloquence, and wit. As Illinois governor, he cleaned up much of the corruption that had dominated the state's politics. He also served as the United States Ambassador to the United Nations and was twice the Democratic Party's candidate for president of the United States.*

- Explain the metaphor in Stevenson's statement.

  ____

  ____

  ____

- Finish the statement with something that is real from your own life or experience.

  It is hard to ______________________________

  if you think you look ______________________________.

- Take a survey of six or more peers. Ask this question:

  "What are you reluctant (or unable) to do, or what is hard for you to do because you are worried about how you would look in the situation?"

  Record some of the answers you get.

  ______________________________ ______________________________

  ______________________________ ______________________________

  ______________________________ ______________________________

  ______________________________ ______________________________

  ______________________________ ______________________________

Name:

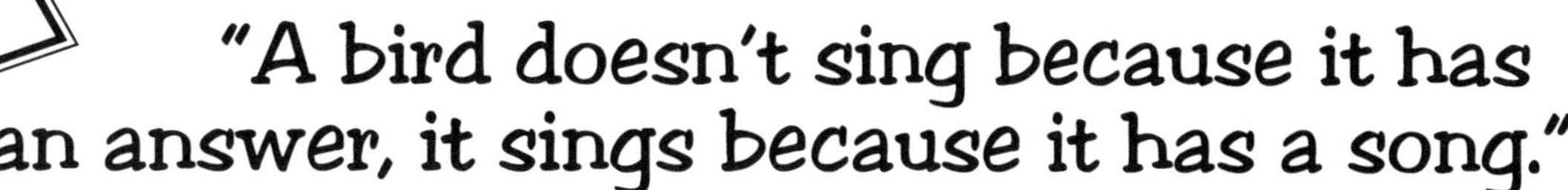

"A bird doesn't sing because it has an answer, it sings because it has a song."

– Maya Angelou

Maya Angelou (1928–) *is an American author, poet, playwright, editor, actress, director, civil rights activist, and teacher. She is best known for the first part of her autobiography,* ***I Know Why the Caged Bird Sings****, which tells the story of a black girl growing up during the Great Depression. In 1993, she became only the second poet in United States history to have the honor of writing and reciting original work at a presidential inauguration.*

- Follow Angelou's literary pattern to say something about **yourself**.

I don't ______________________

because ______________________,

I ______________________

because ______________________.

- Follow Angelou's pattern to say something about **another person or a thing**.

______________ doesn't ______________

because ______________________,

____

because ______________________.

- If Angelou's quote were the refrain in the chorus of a song, what would the first verse of the song be?

____

____

____

____

____

____

____

____

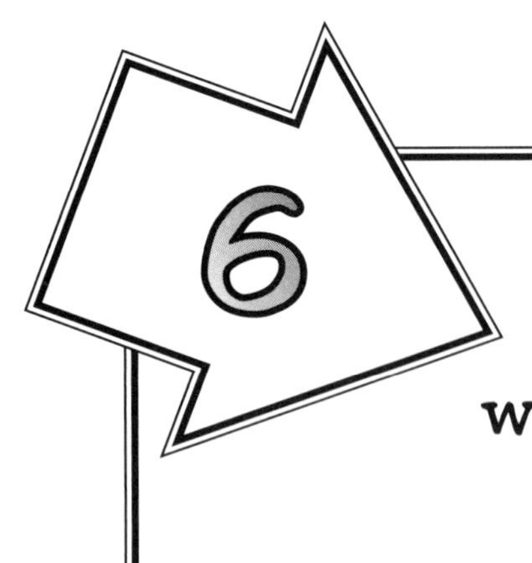

Name: ______________________________

"Lots of people want to ride with you in the limo, but what you want is someone who will take the bus with you when the limo breaks down."

– Oprah Winfrey

Oprah Winfrey (1954–) *is a billionaire and one of the best-known women in the world. She overcame poverty, abuse, and other obstacles to become a broadcaster, movie star, talk show host, activist, and philanthropist. She was honored by* **Time** *magazine as one of the 100 most influential people of the 20th century.*

- What clues does this quote give as to how Ms. Winfrey might feel about her wealth?

  ____
  ____
  ____
  ____
  ____

- Thomas Edison said, *"I have friends in overalls whose friendship I would not swap for the favor of the kings of the world."* What does his message have in common with Oprah's?

  ____
  ____
  ____
  ____

- Join with a partner to discuss attributes and actions that make a good friend. Finish this sentence together.

  Lots of people want to ______________________________ ,

  but what you want is someone who ______________________________

  ______________________________ .

"Being a celebrity doesn't even seem to keep the fleas off our dogs."

– Walt Disney

Walt Disney (1901–1966) *was an American cartoon artist, animator, showman, and film producer. He was noted for his creation of many cartoon characters such as Mickey Mouse and Donald Duck. Disney produced the first animated film with sound,* ***Steamboat Willie****, in 1928. Today, the Walt Disney Company is one of the world's largest media and entertainment conglomerates.*

- Celebrities fascinate most of us. What does this quote cause you to consider about celebrities that you might not have considered before?

  ____

  ____

- What other ordinary problems of life are not erased by fame? Work with a small group to finish this statement in two different ways.

  Being a celebrity doesn't even ____

  ____

  Being a celebrity doesn't even ____

  ____

- Having money can help with a lot of things—but not everything. Sometimes celebrities have problems that do not trouble non-celebrities. Picture or describe something that may be a problem for a celebrity but is not a problem for you (unless you, too, are a celebrity).

Name:

"Ah, but a man's reach should exceed his grasp, or what's a heaven for?"

– Robert Browning

Robert Browning (1812–1889) *was one of the greatest poets of England's Victorian Age. His writings reflect optimism and faith in the value of human life. A famous quote from one of his plays is this: "God's in His heaven—All's right with the world!" Browning's courtship and marriage to Elizabeth Barrett Browning is one of the world's most famous romances.*

- Browning used "heaven" as a metaphor. What is his larger meaning for "heaven" in this quote?

- Some people sense greediness in Browning's line—perhaps suggesting that we should grab for everything we can get, even if it is outside the realistic. Others interpret "grasp" as that which we already hold. How do you interpret Browning's suggestion that "our reach should exceed our grasp"?

- Do you agree that a person's "reach should exceed his grasp"? Tell why or why not.

9

Name:

"Where secrecy or mystery begins, vice or roguery is not far off."

– Samuel Johnson

Samuel Johnson (1709–1784) *was an English poet, essayist, literary critic, editor, and lexicographer. His writings expressed a combination of respect for the past and hope for the future. In 1755, Johnson published* ***A Dictionary of the English Language****, which became one of his greatest accomplishments and had a far-reaching impact on modern English.*

- Meet with a small group. Come to a consensus as to whether you agree or disagree with the quote. Summarize the group's decision.

- Under what circumstances (and to whom) would you tell a secret?

- Should governments and political parties plan schemes in secret? Explain your answer.

- In each bubble, describe a secret that you should keep to yourself.

Name: ______________________________

"Never mistake activity for achievement."

– John Wooden

John Wooden (1910–) *is one of the most successful basketball coaches in history. In his 27 years as coach at UCLA, his team never had a losing season and set a record of 88 consecutive wins. He is the only person to be enshrined in the Basketball Hall of Fame twice—once as a player and once as a coach.*

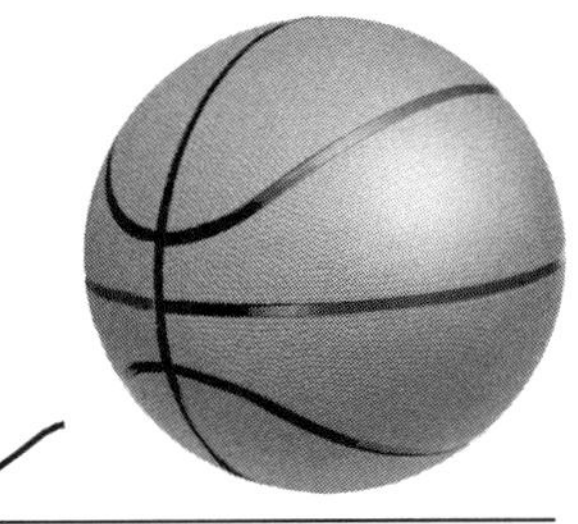

- What do you feel is the difference between achievement and something that is merely activity?

____

____

- What activities might be mistaken for achievement? Use the table below to describe some.

Activity	Why it looks like an achievement	Why it's not an achievement

"There are many words that are like salted jam."

– Turkish proverb

- Use your own words to explain the meaning of this proverb.

- Write some words or phrases "that are like salted jam." Work with a partner if you would like to combine ideas. Include only appropriate expressions.

- Which cartoons on this page use words "that are like salted jam"? Circle the "salty" words or phrases.

"Obstacles cannot crush me; every obstacle yields to stern resolve."

– Leonardo da Vinci

Leonardo da Vinci (1452–1519) *was one of the greatest painters of the Italian Renaissance and of all time. Some of his famous paintings include the* ***Mona Lisa*** *and* ***The Last Supper****. He was also an architect, engineer, mathematician, and philosopher. His keen eye and genius mind led him to make many important scientific discoveries. He recorded all his studies in illustrated notebooks.*

- Define *stern.* ____________________

- Define *resolve.* ____________________

- Obstacles can take many forms, such as poverty, physical or mental disabilities, distance, time, age, or addictions. What "obstacles" do you feel you need to overcome in order to achieve your goals?

____

____

- Think of a fictional (or real) character that overcomes obstacles with "stern resolve." Describe the character briefly. Then list three obstacles that he or she has overcome.

Description: ____________________

Obstacles:

1. ____________________
2. ____________________
3. ____________________

Name: ______________________________

"The frog does not drink up the pond in which he lives."

– Native American proverb

- Who do you think "the frog" is in this metaphor?

  ____

- What do you think "the pond" is in this metaphor?

  ____

- Explain what the metaphor means.

  ____

  ____

- Join with a partner to apply this proverb to yourselves. Assume you are "the frogs" and answer these questions.

  1. *What are some ways you "drink up" your "pond"?*

  ____

  ____

  ____

  2. *What are some ways you could avoid "drinking up" your "pond"?*

  ____

  ____

  ____

Name: ______________________________

"A little learning is a dangerous thing."
– Alexander Pope, English essayist and satirist

"Wisdom begins in wonder."
– Socrates, influential Greek philosopher and teacher

"Some people will never learn anything . . . because they understand everything too soon."
– Alexander Pope, English essayist and satirist

"Learning begins with listening."
– Noah Ben Shea, American poet and comedian-philosopher

- Circle the quote that most catches your interest. Explain your choice.

  ____

- Complete two of the following tasks.

  1. Give an example of an instance where a "little learning" was (or could be) dangerous.

     ____

  2. Complete the following sentences.

     I wonder why my teeth ______________________________ .

     I wonder who will ______________________________ .

     I wonder how ______________________________ **works.**

  3. Give an example of someone who understands everything too soon, and thus does not learn anything. (Do not use real names.)

     ____

Name:

"So live [as if] you wouldn't be ashamed to sell the family parrot to the town gossip."

– Will Rodgers

- What do you think this quote means?

- How might someone live differently if he or she knew that the family's parrot would end up in the hands of the town gossip?

Will Rogers (1879–1935) *was a cowboy movie star who became known not only for his amazing roping skills but for his wisecracks and humorous observations about life. Though he never finished high school, he never stopped learning. He appeared in 71 movies, and wrote six books and 4,000 syndicated newspaper columns.*

- Form a group of three or four people. Imagine a scenario where everyone in town could find out what everyone else was doing and talking about at any time. Discuss what you think would be the negative and positive consequences if this were to happen. Write your ideas below.

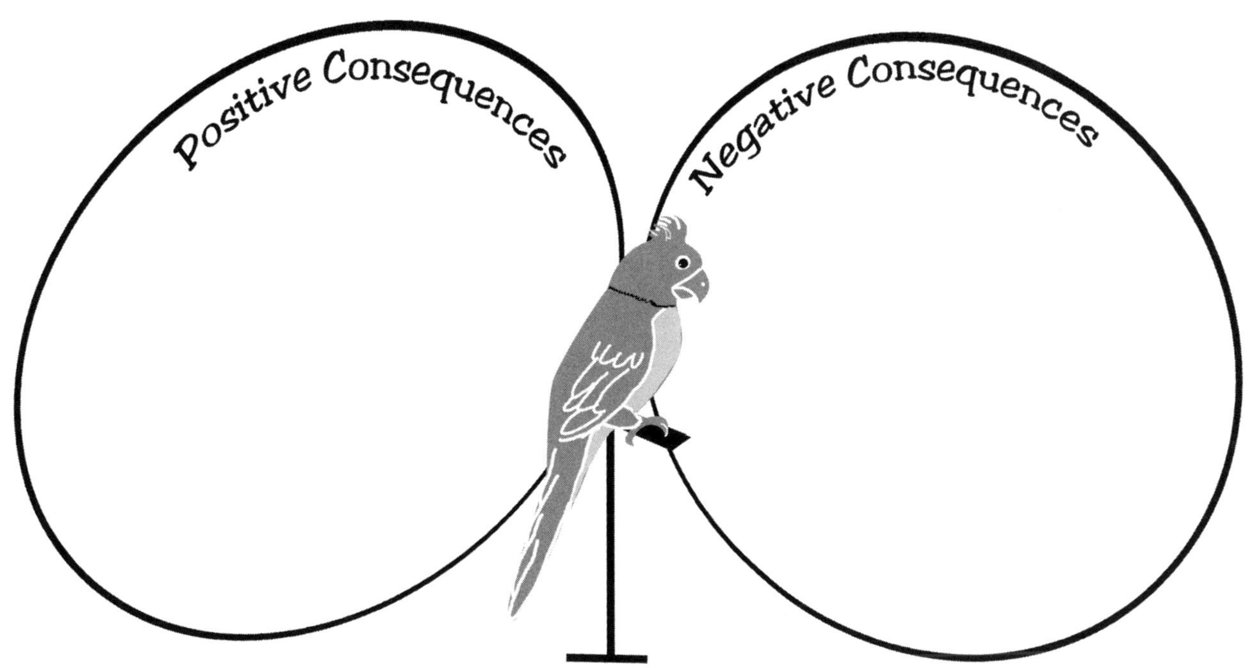

16

Name:

"Figuring out who you are is the whole point of the human experience."

– Anna Quindlen

Anna Quindlen (1952–) *started her journalism career as a copy girl for the* ***New York Times****. She has written fiction, non-fiction, self-help, and children's books, including five bestselling novels. Her work won a Pulitzer Prize in 1992.*

- What experiences in your life so far have helped you figure out who you are?

____

____

____

- What are some things you feel all people should try during their lifetime to help them figure out who they are?

____

____

____

____

- How would you complete this statement?

____ **is**

the whole point of the human experience.

Name: ______________________________

"The trouble with the rat race is that even if you win, you're still a rat."

– Lily Tomlin

Lily Tomlin (1939–) *is an American comedienne, actress, writer, and producer. She has received numerous awards, including six Emmys, two Tonys and a Grammy. Among her best-known roles are the characters she portrayed on the television show* ***Laugh-In****: Ernestine the telephone operator; and Edith Ann, a precocious six year old.*

- How would you define the "rat race"?

  ____

- Why do you think some people spend so much time trying to keep up with others?

  ____

  ____

- Think of something that you originally thought was positive but turned out to be negative. Summarize your experience here. Then share it with one or two others.

  ____

  ____

  ____

- Finish this statement.

  I feel that I am in "the rat race" when ______________________________

  ______________________________.

Name:

"One must never, for whatever reason, turn his back on life."

– Eleanor Roosevelt

Eleanor Roosevelt (1884–1962) *revolutionized the role of First Lady in the United States. Married to President Franklin D. Roosevelt, Eleanor was a strong humanitarian and civil activist. She worked for causes to improve the welfare of women, poor people, youth, and African Americans at home and abroad.*

- What are some ways that a person could "turn his back on life"?

- What are some reasons that someone might "turn his back on life"?

- Briefly describe a time when you felt like "turning your back on life."

Name:

"I am every emotion times ten, I conform yet I'm rebellious, always obeying but somehow still an outlaw, always talking but never heard. I am a teenager."

– Unknown

- What about this quote seems true (or untrue) to you?

- Which of these quotes most sparks your interest?

1. *"You can tell a child is growing up when he stops asking where he came from and starts refusing to tell where he is going." – Unknown*
2. *"Arguing with a teenager is like wrestling in the mud with a pig. Sooner or later you figure out that he/she is enjoying it." – Unknown*
3. *"Never lend your car to anyone to whom you have given birth." – Erma Bombeck, humorist*
4. *"Teenagehood –that time in life when you show your individuality by looking like everyone else." – Unknown*
5. *"I never expected to see the day when girls would get sunburned in the places they do now." – Will Rogers, humorist*
6. *"To an adolescent, there is nothing in the world more embarrassing than a parent." – Dave Barry, humorist*

Explain your choice.

"Two things are infinite: the universe and human stupidity; and I'm not sure about the universe."

– Albert Einstein

The name of **Albert Einstein (1879–1955)** *is synonymous with "genius." Often called "The Father of Physics," Einstein was born in Germany and later lived in Switzerland and the United States. He is best known for his theories of relativity, for which he received a 1921 Nobel Prize in Physics.*

- What is your definition of *stupidity*?

- Do you agree with the quote? Explain your answer.

- List eight things humans do or have done that could be called "stupid."

1. __________
2. __________
3. __________
4. __________
5. __________
6. __________
7. __________
8. __________

- Rate the above eight things on the continuum below. Place each number where you think it belongs.

sort of stupid ←——— pretty stupid ———→ remarkably stupid

Name: ______________________________

"The game isn't over until it's over."

– Yogi Berra

Lawrence (Yogi) Berra (1925–) *is a Baseball Hall-of-Famer who went on to manage the* ***Yankees*** *and the* ***New York Mets****, and to coach the* ***Houston Astros****. Famous also for his cheerful personality, Berra constantly spoke in aphorisms (known as "Yogi-isms") that have made him one of the most quoted personalities of recent history.*

- This famous Berra quote is thought to be about baseball. But, like other "Yogi-isms," it has applications beyond its literal meaning. List some other "games" that could fit this quote.

____

____

____

____

____

____

- Describe a situation (real or fictitious) that demonstrates the truth of Berra's statement.

____

____

____

____

____

- Yogi Berra also said, ***"If you don't know where you are going, you might wind up someplace else."*** Draw a visual representation of this statement.

Name: ______________________________

"If you don't understand yourself, you don't understand anybody else."

– Nikki Giovanni

Nikki Giovanni (1943–) *is an American poet, essayist, and lecturer whose work reflects her pride in her African-American heritage. Her earliest collections of poetry, including* ***Black Feeling, Black Talk****, capture the attitude of the civil rights movement. She has written not only about racism, feminism, and police brutality, but also about love, longing, and loneliness.*

- What do you think it means to "understand" yourself?

  ____

  ____

- What do you think it means to "understand" (or empathize with) someone else?

  ____

  ____

- Do you agree or disagree with Giovanni's quote? ______________

  Give a real-life example to show the reason for your answer to the above question.

  ____

  ____

  ____

23

Name: ______________________________

"The real voyage of discovery consists not in seeking new landscapes, but in having new eyes."

– Marcel Proust

"Things don't change. You change your way of looking, that's all."

– Carlos Castaneda

Marcel Proust (1871–1922), *a French novelist, is often considered one of the greatest writers of the twentieth century. His masterpiece,* ***Remembrance of Things Past****, is a 3,000-page autobiographic novel.*

Carlos Castaneda (1925–1998), *a Peruvian-born American writer, wrote several best-selling books about the mystical teachings of an Indian shaman from Mexico.* **The Teachings of Don Juan** *and other books have sold more than eight million copies in 17 languages.*

- Proust uses metaphors in his quote. Explain one of them.

____

____

____

- Tell another classmate about a time when you had "new eyes" and thus made a discovery.

- Draw a cartoon or sketch that shows the meaning of the Castaneda quote.

Name:

John Cage (1912–1992), *was an innovative and influential American composer of the twentieth century. He experimented with electronic music and unusual musical instruments. One famous composition includes a piece where musicians performed for over four minutes without making a sound. He also contributed to developments in modern dance.*

"I can't understand why people are all frightened by new ideas. I'm frightened by old ones."

– John Cage

- Why might someone be frightened by new ideas?

- Why might someone be frightened by old ideas?

- Briefly describe a new idea you've had that someone ridiculed or denounced.

- Alfonzo is afraid of new ideas. Mazy is afraid of old ideas. Fill in the talk bubbles with a conversation in which Alfonzo tries to convince Mazy that she should hold to an old idea, and Mazy tries to convince Alfonzo of the brilliance of a new idea.

Name: ______________________________

"Don't wait for your ship to come in; swim to it."

– Unknown

- Interview at least three people, including adults. Ask them to tell you what they think this statement means. Summarize their ideas in your own words.

  ____

  ____

  ____

- Answer the questions to describe someone who is always waiting for his or her luck to change, to win the lottery, for a rich uncle to die, or so on.

  What does the person think will be on his or her "ship"? ______________________________

  How does the "waiting" affect that person? ______________________________

  ____

- If you had a "ship coming in," what would be on it? ______________________________

  ____

- What could you do to "swim" to that ship rather than waiting for it to come in?

  ____

- The illustration shows someone ready to swim to her ship. Fill in the balloon to show what she might be thinking.

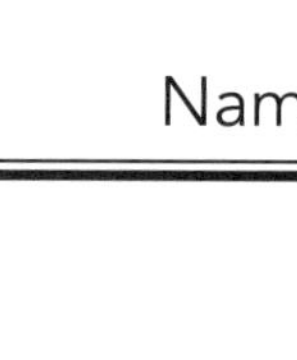

Name: ____________________

"The only fool bigger than the person who knows it all is the person who argues with him."

– Stanislaw J. Lec

Stanislaw J. Lec (1909–1966) *is considered one of Poland's greatest modern writers. His lyrical poems and books of aphorisms, including **Unkempt Thoughts**, contain many philosophical and political messages.*

"The greatest fools are those who do not know they are fools."

– Unknown

- In the talk balloons, write an argument between a fool and a bigger fool (one who argues with the fool).

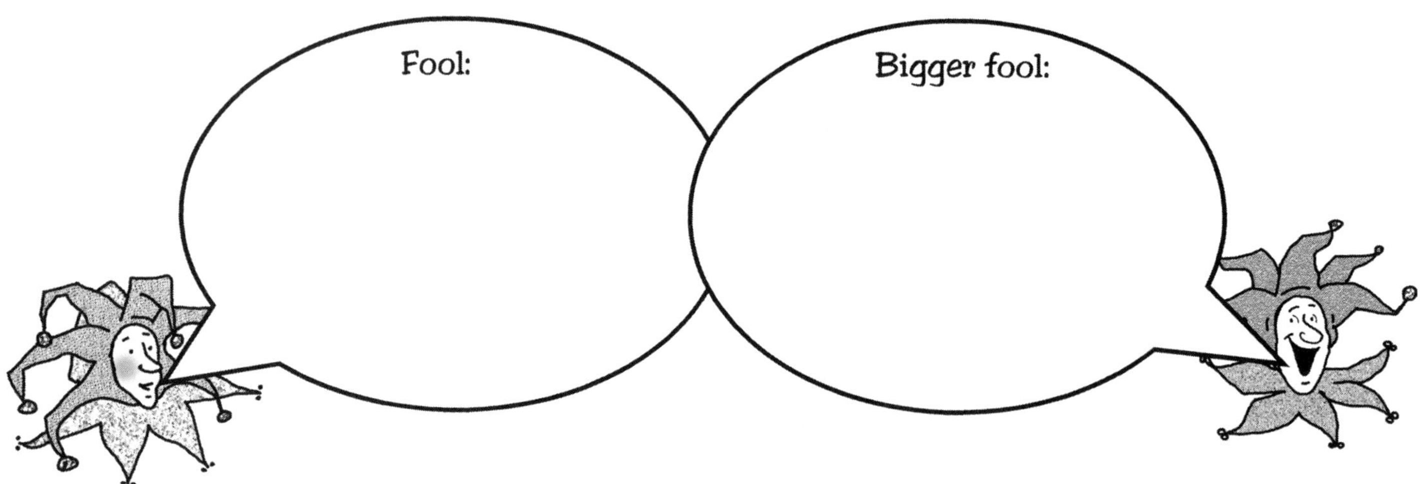

- List three things you would not do if you wanted to avoid being a fool.

1. ____________________ 2. ____________________

3. ____________________

- How can you tell that someone is a fool but does not know that he or she is a fool?

____

____

____

Name: ______________________________

"It costs you something to do good!"

– Zora Neale Hurston

- What do you think Hurston means by "cost" in this statement?

____

____

____

____

Zora Neale Hurston (1891–1960) *was a novelist and folklorist—a leading figure in twentieth century African American literature. She studied anthropology; her stories were influenced by her studies of Southern black folklore. She is best known for her 1937 novel,* ***Their Eyes Were Watching God****, which was made into a movie in 2005.*

- Work with a small group to think of examples of someone doing something "good." Include things that you have done. You can also include things that may not have been done, but could be done in the near future. For each one, identify what the cost of that action has been or probably would be.

Example of doing good	Cost of the action

- Choose one of the examples you wrote. Tell whether or not the cost is worth the action of "doing good." Explain your choice.

____

____

Name:

28

"When you come to the end of your rope, tie a knot and hang on."

– Franklin D. Roosevelt

Franklin D. Roosevelt (1882–1945) *was the 32nd president of the United States and the only one to serve four terms. Though he was afflicted with polio, he refused to let his disability hamper his aspirations. Elected in 1932, he is remembered as the leader who guided America through two of its greatest crises: the Great Depression and World War II.*

- Explain the metaphor in the quote.

- Interview a few people, asking them this question:

  What circumstances have brought you "to the end of your rope"?

  Briefly summarize three of the circumstances people have named.

  1.
  2.
  3.

- Describe a situation in which you have been "at the end of your rope."

- Assume that a friend is terribly distressed because it is almost the end of the semester, and she just can't understand the math she needs to know in order to survive her math class. In this situation, what kind of "knot" could she tie that would help her "hang on"?

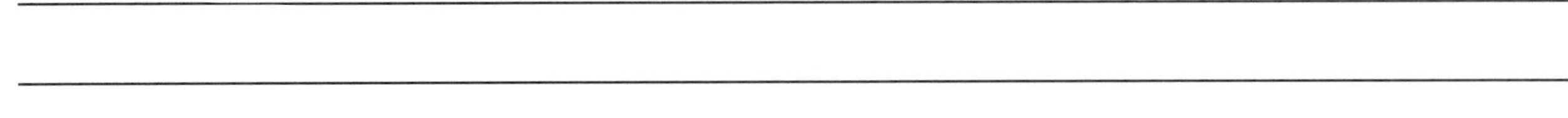

Name: ______________________________

"Fame is a fickle food upon a shifting plate."

– Emily Dickinson

Emily Dickinson (1830–1886) *was one of America's most important and influential poets. She produced more than 1,700 innovative poems (many with strong emotional content) while she lived a socially reclusive life in a small Massachusetts town. She was an accomplished musician and loved language. Her work was not published until after her death.*

- Define *fame.* ______________________________

- Define *fickle.* ______________________________

- Use your own words to explain the meaning of the quote.

  ____

  ____

- Give a present-day example that shows the truth of Dickinson's statement.

  ____

  ____

- Ask a few friends, family members, or classmates to finish the sentence below in a way that shows something insightful about fame.

  Record your top three favorite responses below.

  Fame is ______________________________ .

  Fame is ______________________________ .

  Fame is ______________________________ .

Name: ____________________

"Before you speak, ask yourself: is it kind, is it necessary, is it true, does it improve on the silence?"

– Shirdi Sai Baba

Shirdi Sai Baba (unknown–1918) *was a popular Indian saint who taught a code of love, forgiveness, charity to others, inner peace, and devotion to God. He had little interest in worldly goods. He brought comfort and inspiration to his people; and many still revere him today.*

- Take a survey of ten people. Find out how many of them are comfortable with silence in a discussion or social situation:

☐ **out of ten**

- What important things can result from silence in a conversation, discussion, or other setting?

____

____

____

____

____

- Write something you have said to someone recently or something you would like to say to someone.

- Now test the words in the talk balloon according to Shirdi Sai Baba's quote.

Is it kind? ____________ **Is it necessary to say?** ____________

Is it true? ____________ **Does it improve on silence?** ____________

Name: ______________________________

"If you have enough money, you can see the devil dance."

– German proverb

"Money is a mattress of thorns."

– Maltese proverb

- State the meaning of each proverb in your own words.

  1. ______________________________

  2. ______________________________

- Describe a situation in which you have seen the German proverb to be true.

  ____

  ____

  ____

- Describe a situation in which you have seen the Maltese proverb to be true.

  ____

  ____

  ____

- Work with a partner to finish these proverbs in a new way.

  If you have enough money, ______________________________.

  Money is ______________________________.

  Money is not ______________________________.

"Intelligence without ambition is a bird without wings."

– Salvador Dali

Salvador Dali (1904–1989) *was an imaginative and eccentric Spanish artist who demonstrated his genius in a wide variety of ways. His work included watercolors, drawings, graphics, sculptures, films, photographs, and objects of all descriptions.*

Salvador Dali and friend

- Define *intelligence.* ______________________________

  ____

- Define *ambition.* ______________________________

  ____

- In your own words, explain Dali's metaphorical statement.

  ____

  ____

- Think of someone you know who is intelligent, but is not "flying." (Do not use the real name.)

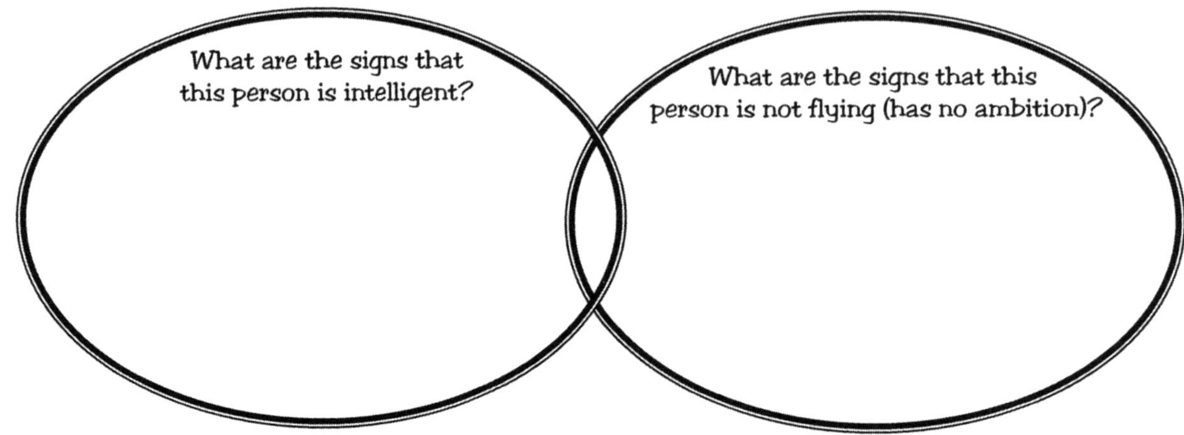

Name:

"You may play with a bull until you get a horn in your eye."

– English proverb

- What do you think the proverb means by "play with a bull"?

- What activities have you seen someone do that could be considered "playing with a bull"?

- Why do you think some people (possibly including yourself) participate in risky activities?

- In your own words, explain the metaphor of "getting a horn in your eye."

Name:

34

"Everything can be taken away from a man but one thing: the last of the human freedoms- to choose one's attitude in any given set of circumstances, to choose one's own way."

– Viktor Frankl

"Freedom is choosing your responsibility. It's not having no responsibilities; it's choosing the ones you want."

– Toni Morrison

Viktor Frankl (1905–1997) *was an Austrian doctor who spent years in four different concentration camps during World War II. His parents, brother, and wife were killed in the camps. During his time there, he tried to cure depression and prevent suicide of fellow prisoners.*

Toni Morrison (1931–) *is a Pulitzer Prize-winning American author, professor, critic, lecturer, and editor. She was also awarded the Nobel Prize for Literature in 1993, and is best known for her powerful and expressive depictions of Black America.*

- From his life experiences, Frankl came to believe that human life has meaning and that a person has some choice, even in situations of unimaginable horror. To what situation in your own life could you apply his idea about freedom?

____

____

____

____

____

____

- Some people think that freedom means you can do anything you want. Toni Morrison gives a different view of freedom. Name three responsibilities that you freely choose or want to choose in the future.

1. ______________________________

2. ______________________________

3. ______________________________

Name:

"The mouse that has but one hole is soon caught."

– Arabian proverb

- Explain the metaphor in the proverb.

  ____

- Finish the limerick.

> There once was a mouse named Levatt
>
> Who was spied by a troublesome __________
>
> To his one hole he ran
>
> But ______________________________
>
> And ______________________________

- There is rarely just one solution to a problem. The more options you have, the better. Think of two different solutions to each of these problems.

A You don't have enough money to buy something you really want.

1. ______________________________
2. ______________________________

B You feel that your life is too busy (school, athletics, activities, etc.)

1. ______________________________
2. ______________________________

C Your friend always borrows things (or money) from you and never gives them back.

1. ______________________________
2. ______________________________

Name:

"Men have become the tools of their tools."

– Henry David Thoreau

- Fill the toolbox with sketches or words naming several "tools" that humans use today. Be sure to include "tools" that **you** use.

Henry David Thoreau (1817–1862) *was an American author, poet, philosopher, and naturalist who criticized many of the social and political conventions of his day. For nearly two years, he lived alone in a small house near Walden Pond and recorded many observations on nature and people. His best-known book,* ***Walden****, is a chronicle of these experiences.*

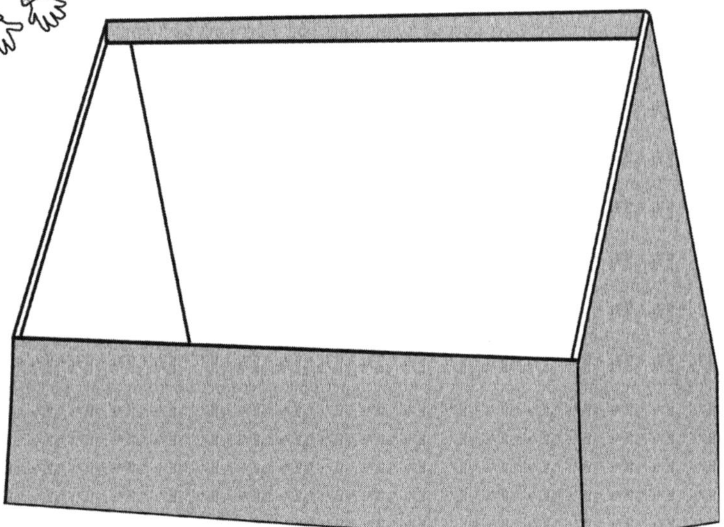

- Choose four of the tools in your toolbox. Complete the table below.

Name of Tool	How does it make your life easier or more convenient?	How does it "use" you? How do you become a tool of it?

Name: ______________________________

"Before you embark on a journey of revenge, dig two graves."

– Confucius

- Define *revenge*. ______________________________

____

____

- Why does Confucius tell you to dig two graves?

____

____

____

- Give an example that you have observed or experienced in which someone embarked on a journey of revenge." (Do not use real names.)

____

____

____

Confucius (551–479 BC) *was a Chinese philosopher whose teachings of morality, justice, honesty, and social correctness influenced much of Asian life and culture. Many aphorisms (short proverbs or bits of wisdom) have been collected in* ***The Analects*** *of Confucius.*

- In the example you described above, how did the person with revenge in mind actually move toward "burying" herself or himself?

____

____

____

____

"Poetry is opening a can of yourself."

– Lucy Bridges, middle school student

"Poetry always goes straight to the marrow."

– Edna O'Brien, Irish author, poet, playwright, author of *Johnny I Hardy Knew You*

"As an individual process, I see it [poetry] as a way to delve into the self."

– Georgia Popoff, American poet, author of *Coaxing Nectar from Longing*

- Finish the statement in your own way.

  Poetry is ____.

- Expressing your emotions in the form of poetry or reading someone else's poetry is often helpful in times when you must deal with difficult issues. Name a poet whose poetry can help you to think about your own life.

  ____

- Poetry often brings out emotions. What poem has triggered laughter, tears, anger, or other strong emotion for you?

  ____

- Our deepest feelings sometimes pour forth on paper more easily than we can speak them. Finish the poem to express some feelings that are important to you.

  When I am relieved, I feel like ______________________________.

  When I am angry, I ______________________________________.

  I can't stop smiling when __________________________________.

  When ______________________________, **I just wanted to be alone.**

Name:

"There is no such thing as part freedom."

– Nelson Mandela

Nelson Rolihlahla Mandela (1918–) *was the leader of an anti-apartheid activist movement in South Africa who was convicted of sabatoge against the government and served 27 years in prison. He helped negotiate the beginning of a democracy in South Africa, and was a key participant in helping to heal the nation's wounds, eventually becoming the country's president. He received many awards for his work towards peace, democracy, and reconciliation—including the 1993 Nobel Peace Prize.*

- What do you think Nelson Mandela meant by "part freedom"?

- Do you agree with his statement? Explain your answer.

- Briefly describe five things you believe are aspects of "full" freedom.

1.
2.
3.
4.
5.

Name: ____________________

"Never try to teach a pig to sing. It wastes your time and annoys the pig."

– Lazarus Long

Lazarus Long *is a character in the 1973 novel,* ***Time Enough for Love*** *by Robert A. Heinlein. In the novel, Lazarus has a collection of witty sayings and bits of wisdom written in notebooks.*

- Give your interpretation of the deeper meaning of the quote.

____

____

____

- Finish the following two lists.

10 Things *Never* to Try

1. ____________________
2. ____________________
3. ____________________
4. ____________________
5. ____________________
6. ____________________
7. ____________________
8. ____________________
9. ____________________
10. ____________________

10 Things You *Should* Try

1. ____________________
2. ____________________
3. ____________________
4. ____________________
5. ____________________
6. ____________________
7. ____________________
8. ____________________
9. ____________________
10. ____________________

Name:

41

"Discontent is the first necessity of progress."

– Thomas Edison

Thomas Edison (1847–1931) *was one of the most prolific inventors in world history. During his lifetime, he received more than 1,000 patents for his innovations, including the electric light bulb, the phonograph, and the motion picture camera.*

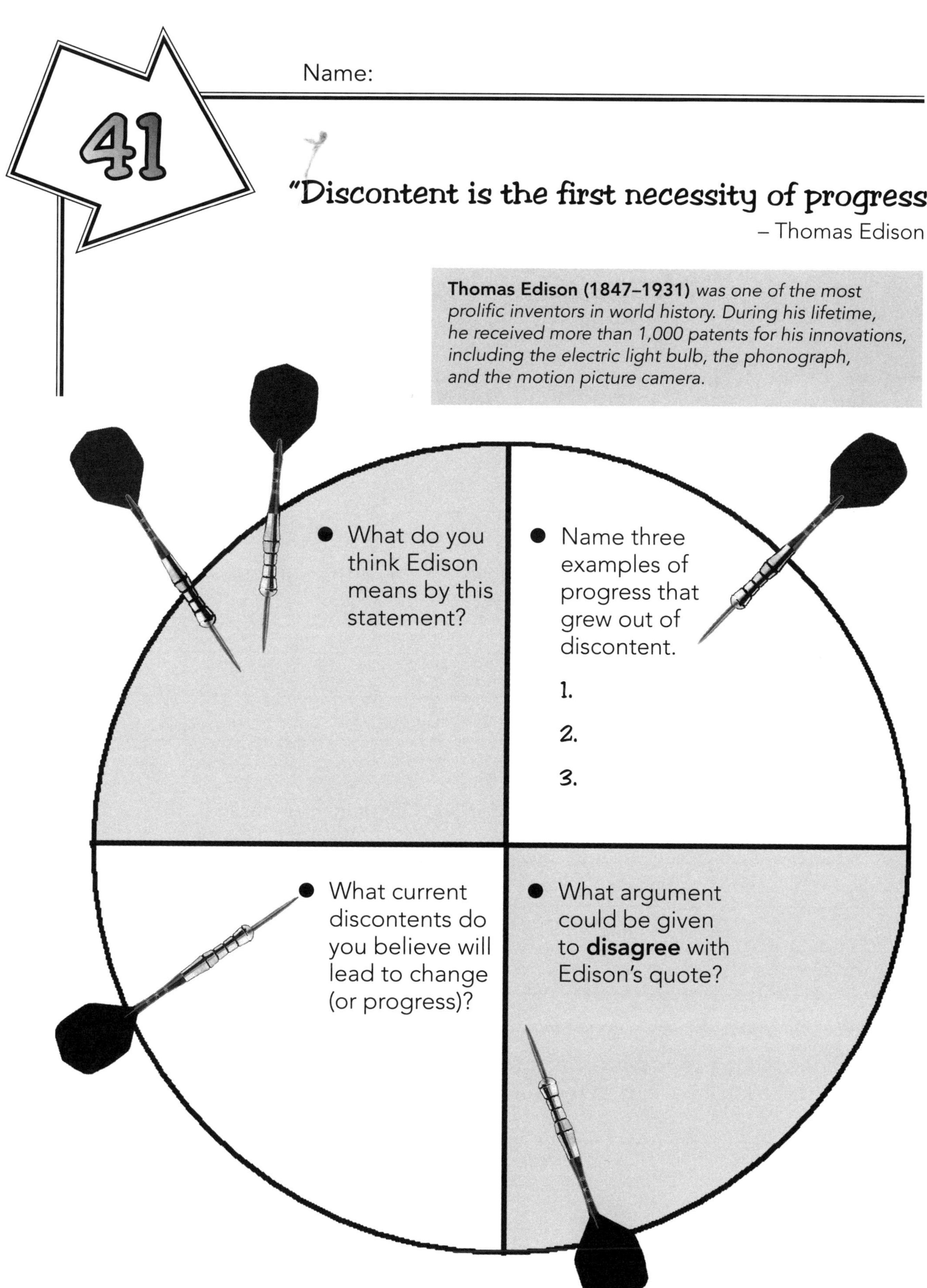

- What do you think Edison means by this statement?

- Name three examples of progress that grew out of discontent.

1.

2.

3.

- What current discontents do you believe will lead to change (or progress)?

- What argument could be given to **disagree** with Edison's quote?

Name:

"We're all in this together."

– Unknown

"We are all in this together—by ourselves."

– Lily Tomlin

Lily Tomlin (1939–) *is known as one of America's funniest women. She is a successful comedienne and award-winning TV, movie, and stage actress.*

- What do you think the authors of these quotes meant by "this"?

- Circle the quote above that is most true for you. Explain your choice.

- If you were writing a song with one of these quotes as the title, what would the last two lines of the song be?

Name: ______________________________

"Fashion is for people who need someone else to tell them who they are."

– Kacey Adams, high school student

- Explain why you believe this statement is true (or not true).

  ____

  ____

- Circle the fashion quote that is most interesting to you.

"What a strange power there is in clothing."
– Isaac Singer, inventor

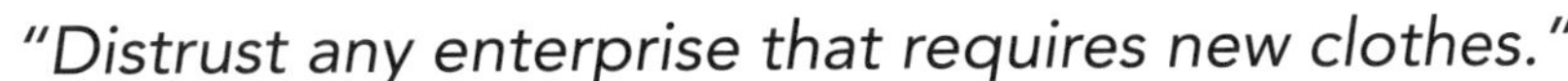

"Distrust any enterprise that requires new clothes."
– Henry David Thoreau, social critic

"The truly fashionable are beyond fashion."
– Cecil Baton, fashion photographer

"I base my fashion sense on what doesn't itch."
– Gilda Radner, humorist

"Never wear anything that panics the cat."
– P. J. O'Rourke, political satirist

"It's always the badly-dressed people who are the most interesting."
– Jean Paul Gaultier, fashion designer

- Explain your choice.

  ____

- Describe or draw a fashion item or outfit that "defines" a person who would wear it.

Name: ______________________

"You may be disappointed if you fail, but you are doomed if you don't try."

– Beverly Sills

Beverly Sills (1929–) *is one of the most beloved and respected opera sopranos of the 20th century. She performed in the world's leading opera houses, won many awards for her record albums and TV program, "Lifestyles with Beverly Sills," and published a best-selling autobiography,* ***Bubbles: A Self-Portrait****. She was also national chair of the March of Dimes' Mothers' March on Birth Defects and chairwoman of New York's Metropolitan Opera.*

- What do you think Beverly Sills means by "you are doomed"?

  ____

  ____

- How does it feel to fail at something?

  ____

  ____

- Give an example **to support** the idea in this quote.

  ____

  ____

  ____

  ____

- Some people argue that it is important to experience failure—that failure makes you a stronger, better person. Give one argument **in opposition** to this idea.

  ____

  ____

  ____

Name: ____________________

"The best way to destroy an enemy is to make him your friend."

– Abraham Lincoln

Captain Kirk embraces his enemy, a Klingon.

Abraham Lincoln (1809–1865) *was the 16th president of the United States. His presidency was occupied mainly with the Civil War conflict. He was a great statesman and considered to be one of the country's greatest presidents. He also had a passion for reading and learning and is known for his wise, insightful statements.*

- Abraham Lincoln's quote contains a paradox. What is paradoxical about Lincoln's statement?

____

____

____

- How would you go about making an enemy into a friend? Join with a partner to identify at least two strategies you could use.

1. ____________________
2. ____________________

- High school principal Paul Gasparini said, *"When you get to know the other person, they are no longer the other."* Briefly describe an example that shows the truth of this statement.

____

____

- During a summit meeting between President Mikhail Gorbachev of the former Soviet Union and former President Ronald Reagan, a Soviet representative said, *"We are going to do something terrible to you; we are going to deprive you of an enemy."* Why do you suppose some people or nations "need" enemies?'

____

____

Name:

"Love makes your soul crawl out from its hiding place."

– Zora Neale Hurston

- How does a person act when his or her soul is in a "hiding place"?

- What do you think causes people to "hide their souls"?

Zora Neale Hurston (1891–1960) *was a novelist, folklorist, and anthropologist during the time of America's Harlem Renaissance. Of her novels, short stories, plays, and essays, she is best known for her 1937 work* ***Their Eyes Were Watching God.***

- Finish the statement in your own way.

- In the space above, create a cartoon or other visual to show the literal or metaphorical meaning of this quote.

Name: ______________________________

"Jealousy is the jaundice of the soul."
– John Dryden, English poet

"Jealousy is all the fun you think they had . . ."
– Erica Jong, American author and teacher

"Jealousy, that dragon which slays love under the pretense of keeping it alive."
– Havelock Ellis, English social reformer

"Envy eats nothing but its own heart."
– German proverb

"Oh, what a bitter thing it is to look into happiness through another man's eyes!"
– William Shakespeare, English poet and playwright

I'M GREEN WITH ENVY!

- Define *jaundice*.

  ____

  ____

- Define *pretense*.

  ____

  ____

- What does Ellis mean when he says that "jealousy slays love"?

  ____

  ____

  ____

- Finish the statement below:

  The long-lasting effect of envy is ____________

  ______________________________.

- Briefly describe a time when you were jealous of someone, then discovered that what the person had was not so desirable after all.

  ____

  ____

  ____

  ____

  ____

  ____

Name: ________________________________

"No snowflake in an avalanche ever feels responsible."

– Stanislaw J. Lec

Stanislaw J. Lec (1909–1966) *is considered one of Poland's greatest modern writers. His lyrical poems and books of aphorisms, including* ***Unkempt Thoughts****, contain many philosophical and political messages.*

- Explain Lec's metaphor in your own words.

____

____

- Join with a small group to think of real-life examples that show the truth of Lec's idea. Write two of them here.

1. ________________________________

2. ________________________________

- When have you been a "snowflake" that has become part of a bigger problem?

____

____

____

____

- Write a caption for the cartoon.

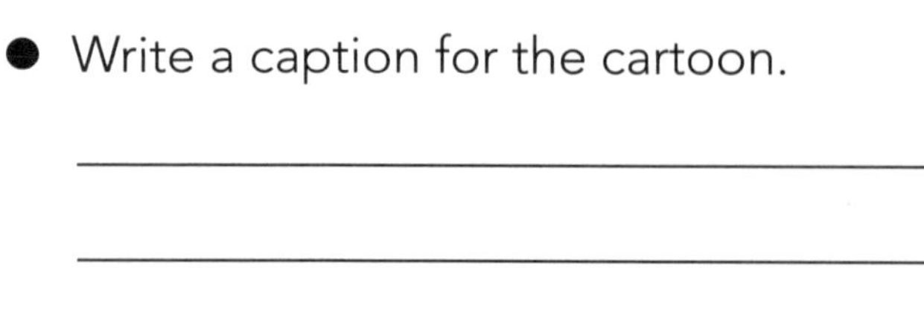

____

____

____

Name: ______________________

"I have found that, among its other benefits, giving liberates the soul of the giver."

– Maya Angelou

"Taking makes me feel like I'm dying. Giving makes me feel like I'm living."

– Mitch Albom

Maya Angelou (1928–) *is a novelist, poet, dancer, actor, professor, and activist. Among her most famous works are* ***I Know Why the Caged Bird Sings*** *and the poem, "On the Pulse of Morning."*

Mitch Albom (1958–) *started his career as a sportswriter and musician, and went on to become a best-selling and award-winning author, journalist, screenwriter, and playwright.*

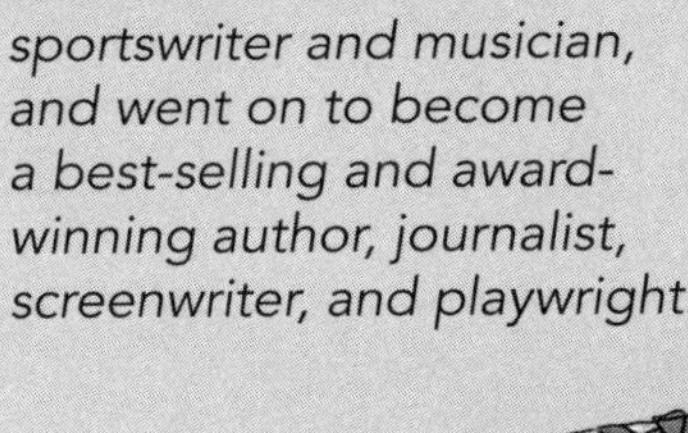

- Give three examples of "taking."

1. ______________________

2. ______________________

3. ______________________

- Give three examples of "giving."

1. ______________________

2. ______________________

3. ______________________

- Interview one other person. Ask him or her to finish one statement in each group (giving and taking). Write the responses. Finish the other two statements yourself.

Giving makes me feel like ______________________

____

______________________.

Giving ______________________

____

______________________.

Taking makes me feel like ______________________.

Taking ______________________.

Name: ____________________

"Who will take responsibility for raising the next generation?"

– Ruth Bader Ginsburg

"Today's teenagers are raising themselves and each other."

– Anna Manches

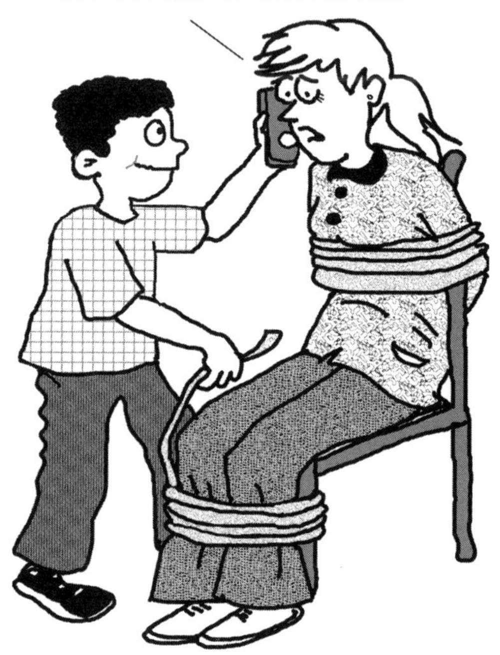

Ruth Bader Ginsburg (1933–) *is a current justice (since 1993) on the United States Supreme Court—one of three women ever to serve on this high court.*

Anna Manches (1996–) *is a high school freshman who wrote this statement as the theme sentence for an essay in a cultural studies class.*

- What might lead someone to ask the question that Ginsburg asked?

____

____

- Do you agree with Anna's statement? __________ Explain your answer.

____

____

- Meet with a partner to create some pieces of advice for parents who are trying to raise teenagers. Write your best creation here.

____

____

Name:

"All progress has resulted from people who took unpopular decisions."

– Adlai Stevenson

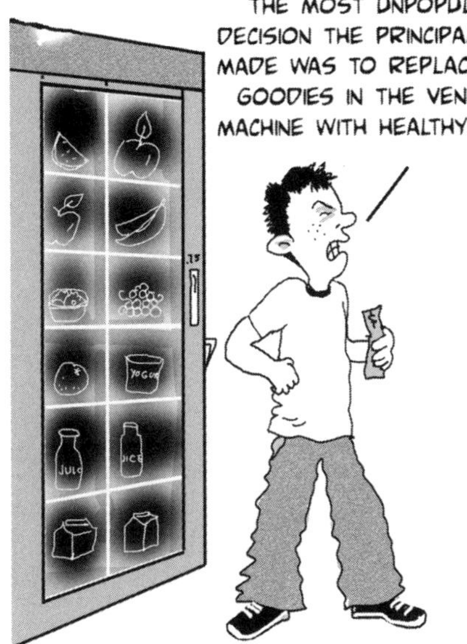

Adlai Stevenson (1900–1965) *was an American political leader and statesman. His chief interest was foreign affairs and he served as a United Nations delegate for two years. He was a governor of Illinois and twice ran for president of the United States. Though he did not win, he remained very influential in the country.*

- Give three examples of progress that resulted from someone who took an unpopular decision.

Unpopular decision	Progress that resulted from it
1.	
2.	
3.	

- The "Bill of Rights," part of the *United States Constitution*, grants all citizens the right to freedom of speech, even if the message is not one that most people want to hear. Why is it important that unpopular decisions not be banned?

- Stevenson says "all progress" results from unpopular decisions. Is this true? Join a few other people to try to think of an example of progress that did not result from an unpopular decision.

Name:

"It is easier to forgive an enemy than to forgive a friend."

– William Blake

William Blake (1757–1827) *was an influential British poet and artist whose work valued imagination over reason. He was a nonconformist who went against the conventions of his time, determined not to sacrifice his vision in order to become popular.*

- Take a survey of ten people. Ask them, **"Is it easier to forgive an enemy or to forgive a friend?"** Record your survey results.

______________ **said it is easier to forgive a friend.**

______________ **said it is easier to forgive an enemy.**

- Does anything about the results of your survey surprise you? If so, what?

____

____

- Give an argument **in support** of Blake's quote.

____

____

____

- Give an argument **in opposition** to Blake's quote.

____

____

____

Name: ______________________________

"A man who carries a cat by the tail learns something he can learn in no other way."

"If you pick up a starving dog and make him prosperous, he will not bite you. This is the principle difference between a dog and a man."

"Let us not be too particular. It is better to have old second-hand diamonds than none at all."

– Quotes by Mark Twain

Mark Twain (1835–1910), *whose real name was Samuel Clemens, was a great author and humorist. His wise and witty sayings have made him one of America's most-quoted authors. He is remembered for his social criticism and cynical view of the human race.*

- Explain the metaphor in each quote.

1. ______________________________
____
____

2. ______________________________
____
____

3. ______________________________
____
____

WHAT'S HIS PROBLEM?

- Circle the quote that seems most true. Give a real-life example to show the truth of the idea.

____
____
____

Name:

"Man who stand on hill with mouth open will wait long time for roast duck to drop in."

– Confucius

- Write a caption for the cartoon.

  ____

  ____

- What do you think this proverb means?

  ____

  ____

  ____

Confucius (551–479 BC) *was a Chinese philosopher whose teachings influenced much of Asian life and culture. From a young age he displayed an extraordinary love of learning and appreciation for his country. His philosophy and aphorisms emphasize the importance of human virtues such as morality, modesty, honesty, and thoughtfulness.*

- Give a real-life example to show the meaning of this proverb.

  ____

  ____

  ____

  ____

Name: ______________________________

"Never let a fool kiss you, or a kiss fool you."

– Joey Lauren Adams

Joey Lauren Adams (1971–) *is an American actress, writer, and director. Known for her high-pitched speaking voice, she has appeared in more than thirty movies and television shows.*

- Survey five adults and five kids, asking them each these three questions:

  1. Have you ever been fooled by a kiss?

  2. Have you ever kissed a fool?

  3. What lesson did you learn from either of these experiences?

- Record your results.

Number of adults fooled by a kiss	Number of kids fooled by a kiss	Number of adults kissed by a fool	Number of kids kissed by a fool

- Write the best answer to question number 3.

____

____

____

- Which is worse—to be fooled by a kiss or kissed by a fool? Explain your answer.

____

____

Teacher Notes

Additional information or activities for each of the following quotes (by quote number):

1. Brainstorm real-life examples of situations (personal, current events, or historical), in which an enemy stimulated an action. Discuss the consequences of the action.

2. The epigram—one of Ogden Nash's best-known poetic forms, is a short pithy saying, usually in verse, often with a quick, satirical twist at the end. The subject is usually a single thought or event. Track down other Nash epigrams and encourage students to try writing their own.

3. Share excerpts from Bruce Coville books with students. Encourage students to write and illustrate their own stories about aliens, monsters, dragons, and other Coville subjects.

4. Check out these two resources about students and self-confidence: an article at **http://www.nmsa.org/Publications/MiddleGround/Articles/October2007/Article1/tabid/1510/Default.aspx** and a lesson plan at **http://school.discoveryeducation.com/lessonplans/programs/selfesteem/**.

5. Maya Angelou recited the poem "On the Pulse of Morning" at President Clinton's inauguration (January 19, 1993). For an interesting interdisciplinary activity, discuss how this poet reflected her political views through this verse.

6. Follow up the tasks on this page with a class discussion where students share their varied impressions of Oprah Winfrey. (Most students are familiar with at least some aspect of her work.)

7. Most students never consider the downsides of fame. Have students work in small groups to make a chart with the "pros" on one side and the "cons" on the other and see where it leads.

8. This quote is taken from Browning's poem, "Andrea del Sarto." In this dramatic monologue spoken in the voice of a Renaissance painter, the artist compares his own work to that of the master painters of his time. Find the text at **http://www.poemhunter.com/poem/andrea-del-sarto**.

9. Define *vice* and *roguery*. Brainstorm examples of both. Samuel Johnson was one of the first to compile a dictionary. Ask students how they think today's dictionaries are put together and who decides what goes in them. Visit **http://www.merriam-webster.com**.

10. Coach John Wooden has his own website filled with inspirational stories and quotes. Visit **www.coachwooden.com.**

11. It can be argued that anything is a right answer to the final task. Students must support their choices with explanations as to why the words they circle are "like salted jam."

12. Students may be interested in seeing pictures of Da Vinci's most famous works—as well as those many other works that are not as well known.

13. Introduce students to key figures in environmental movements, so that they can search for other quotes about taking care of their own habitat.

14. Let these quotes spark a discussion about learning and schools in general. Ask students to consider what might happen if Americans didn't have access to public education (and why).

15. The Will Rogers Memorial Museum maintains a website full of resources and lesson ideas. It is available at **http://www.willrogers.com.**

Additional information or activities for each of the following quotes (by quote number):

16. Use this quote in advisory programs, character education lessons, and other places where students can discuss what it means to "find yourself" or "know yourself."

17. Stimulate thinking and integrate disciplines by launching a discussion about how the "rat race" has changed throughout history. (For instance, consider how technology has changed the meaning and nature of the "rat race.")

18. Introduce students to the term *resilience* and share examples of this trait. Ask students to hypothesize about why some people seem to be more resilient than others.

19. Have students write individual or small-group poems or paragraphs about what it means to them to be a teenager. They can also interview parents or older friends and ask their opinions.

20. Einstein is known as a genius. Ask students to consider whether he would include himself in this assessment of human stupidity. (They may need to investigate other Einstein quotes to gather evidence for their conclusions.)

21. A complete list of "Yogi-isms" is available at **http://www.yogiberra.com/yogi-isms.html**.

22. Students might enjoy hearing some poems from her collection *Hip Hop Speaks to Children: A Celebration of Poetry with a Beat* (2008). The book comes with a CD.

23. Have two students volunteer to sit in front of the class, back-to-back, and take turns describing what they see. It can be a good concrete reminder of perspective and how looking at something in a new way can change everything.

24. Students may want to do further research about John Cage's controversial composition, "Four Minutes Thirty-Three Seconds." It can lead to interesting discussions about the nature of art and music.

25. Use the quote to spark a discussion of familiar metaphors. Ask students to gather or create other "ship" and "water" metaphors. Explain to students that, when ships were the only means of transportation over water, it sometimes took months for supplies to reach the New World.

26. Students will enjoy writing their own aphorisms about fools. They can finish such sentences as
The greatest fools are ______________;
You can tell a fool by ______________;
The only fool bigger than the person who __________is the person who __________.

27. Begin a discussion about the "cost" of philanthropy. Students can think of or research philanthropists and examine or infer the "costs" they may have paid for their work.

28. Students can write other "end-of-your-rope" scenarios, then share them with other students who suggest "knots" that can help someone in the situation "hang on."

29. In addition to its metaphorical images, this quote provides an excellent example of alliteration. Students can try writing metaphors that include alliteration, personification, or other literary devices.

30. Ask students to create bits of advice to give to younger students, beginning with the phrase, "Before you speak..."

31. Money is a great topic for proverbs and other aphorisms. Students can create completely original proverbs or bits of advice about money.

32. Introduce students to Dali's art style by showing them pictures of his work. Then they might try to create a visual representation of the idea in the quote, mimicking Dali's style.

33. This quote can spark discussions about some controversial behavior subjects such as drug and alcohol use.

34. Use this quote to begin a cross-discipline lesson about the nature of freedom as a founding principle of America.

35. Ask students to comment on the meanings of other quotes and proverbs about mice: "A shy cat makes a proud mouse;" "The mouse is a mistress in her own house;" and "If you build a better mousetrap, you will catch better mice."

36. Examine benefits and consequences of technology. Students can list several technological inventions and discuss how each one helps and hinders society or individuals.

Additional information or activities for each of the following quotes (by quote number):

37. Ask students to search for other advice related to revenge or to write their own aphorisms about revenge.

38. This page is an excellent opening for a poetry unit. Have students bring in favorite poems of their own (written by them or not) as examples to show the truth of these quotes.

39. Give students a brief overview of South Africa's history so that they understand the context for this quote. Explain *apartheid*, the attempts at reforms to *apartheid* in the 1980s (attempting to give "part freedom"), the eventual end to *apartheid*, and the role Mandela and others played in moving toward democracy for all South Africans.

40. Challenge students to give real-life examples of someone "trying to teach a pig to sing."

41. Students can prepare a few strong arguments (with examples) that agree or disagree with the statement and hold a casual debate.

42. Challenge students to use music, dance, drawing, mime, or other non-verbal means to communicate one of the quotes.

43. Use this page to begin an exploration of fashion, especially related to certain times in history. Explore these sites: **http://www.pbs.org/newshour/infocus/fashion/whatisfashion.html** and **http://www.fashion-era.com**.

44. Share a recording of Beverly Sills' singing. Many students will be unfamiliar with opera—and hers is a voice they should experience!

45. Explain the term *paradox* (a statement that, though often true, contains a contradiction). Then use this quote as a springboard for discussions on friendship and peer relationships in middle school.

46. There are countless quotes, proverbs, and aphorisms about love. Students can collect and illustrate their favorites.

47. Jealousy and envy are strong parts of the human experience. Teenagers and pre-teenagers know this well. Distinguish between the two and ask students to suggest some workable remedies for jealousy and envy.

48. Use this to start a discussion about personal responsibility. Students will also enjoy a related story found at **http://www.starrbrite.com/starfish.html**.

49. Expand personal response to the quotes by asking students to give words, phrases, or examples to answer these questions:
1) What does it mean to "feel like you're dying"?
2) What does it mean to "feel like you're living"?

50. Ask students to discuss this question: "Who SHOULD take responsibility for raising the next generation?"

51. Decide, as a group, to become alert to progress. Keep identifying examples of progress that you see, bring those examples to class, share them, and examine whether or not that particular kind of progress resulted from an unpopular decision.

52. Discuss forgiveness. Ask students to work together to write advice on how to forgive a friend.

53. Mark Twain can be the subject of a variety of lessons and units, from literature to history to the Mississippi River. An interesting biographical video, entitled *Mark Twain: His Amazing Adventures* (1995), will provide background information.

54. Visit this website for a Confucius biography and more sayings: **http://www.confucius.org/main01.htm**.

55. Discuss answers to the final question on the page. You add your opinion to the discussion. As a part of the discussion, you might ask students to define what they mean (in this context) by a "fool."